Thank You For

Firing Me and Letting Me G(reatest) O(pportunity)

D. Wilson, Sr.

Through It All Publishing—Aurora, CO
ISBN: 979-8-218-35351-3
Library of Congress Control Number: 2024902272
Title: *Thank You For Firing Me and Letting Me G(reatest)O(pportunity)*
Author: D. Wilson, Sr.
Digital distribution | 2024
Paperback | 2024

Dedication

I would first like to thank my wife for her support and time for helping me. I would also like to dedicate this book to all the employers that fired me, because this has motivated me to find my purpose with the help from God.

Table of Contents

Introduction.. vii
Phase 1 1
Phase 2 7
Phase 3 10
Jobs 13
Phase 4 32
Phase 5 42
Phase 6 44
Phase 7 49
Phase 8 62
Phase 9 69
Phase 10 76
Human Resources 82
The Saboteurs 83
The Critics 85
The Fearful Ones 87
The Supporter 88

Introduction

This book is about the journey that I have been through of being fired by companies in the corporate world, whether it is because of politics, favoritism, or finding a reason to let me go. I am writing to tell you about a different type of situation that I believe everyone may have experienced. But if no one has had these experiences, it is ok. I am sharing these experiences so that it will help someone and provide insight of what I have seen and been through. I realize not everyone will understand or relate. I tell everything that is good, bad and indifferent. I talk about jobs, Human Resources, The Saboteurs, The Critics, The Supporters, The Fearless Ones. In this book I will talk about some people I have come across that have made these experiences exciting for me to write about. If you have ever been fired from a job I encourage you to keep pressing on and make a change. Look in the mirror and check to make sure you are not the problem and do something about it. I did not want to keep going through the same thing. So I stepped out in faith and changed my career and even until now things have turned around. If I can do it you can too. Enjoy the reading of this book.

God bless you.

D. Wilson, Sr.

Phase 1

Hello, and thank you for getting this book to read. If you experienced getting fired from a job this book is for you. Throughout my life of working, I have been fired from more than one job and not because it has been my fault. It has always been either because, business closing down, downsizing, or the excuse of it being a performance issue but the real reason is because of who I am and that I don't go out for drinks, smoke marijuana or hang out after work. But I noticed that it was becoming a trend and once people would see that all I wanted to do is come to work and not get caught up in their mess or gossip, they would find different ways to separate themselves and use whatever excuse and tactics to get me fired from a job by doing it undercover.

As a man of faith, I have worked different jobs that did not work out from fields like Customer Service, Collections, Call Centers, Financial Services, even Retail and some of these jobs I would be at for several years. When I did get fired I felt like I was encouraged and inspired and knew God would bless me with better. Thank you for letting me G(reatest) O(pportunity). I looked at this as the Greatest Opportunity to do something different and make a change which is why I wanted to write about it and turn it around for my good which may also help somebody else.

Most people would feel embarrassed, sad, not

worthy, lowlife, worrying about how they are going to pay their bills and might have to file for unemployment and start all over. I get it about starting all over again that's never easy. But I will tell you after going through these experiences. I did need help and the help that I needed was to first turn to God. I told myself that enough is enough. This is the last time I will get fired from a job. During my time off work, I would pray and fast which was great for me to get focused and draw closer to God.

I would pray every day and take communion and stand on God's word that he would bless me with better job opportunities. I would read scriptures like (Psalms 37:25 - I have been young, and now am old, yet I have not seen the righteous forsaken nor his descendants begging bread). (1 John 4:4 - You are of God, little children and have overcome them, because He who is in you is greater than he who is in the world). (Psalms 37:23 - The steps of a good man are ordered by the Lord, And he delights in his way). I also have looked into wanting to start my own business. I have taken some courses online to keep myself occupied. I also have been listening to this Motivational Speaker named Eric Thompson who has been very motivating to me. I would recommend everybody to listen to him. I tell you this man has helped me by speaking into my life. He has mentioned some things in his messages that have inspired me to see how I myself can be successful. Not only that, we have some similar things in life that I can relate to, like how he has been married for over 30 plus years and how his wife is his high school sweetheart. But I will say that if you are feeling like giving up don't do it, find ways that are going to help you get over this temporary hump. Learn other ways to keep your focus. There is a saying that says, "There is a light at the end of the tunnel."

I realized that every time that I have been fired from a job it was getting me one step closer to where God wanted me to be or see. In (John 16:33 - These things I have spoken to you, that in Me you may have peace, in the world you will have tribulation, but be of good cheer, I have overcome the world). At one time when I was not working I went to get a couple of thank you cards to send to the companies that I have been fired from. One person may think to themselves please or I don't care and I am not wasting my time and to keep it moving. I am doing this for myself, I don't care if they get the card, look at it or throw it away, but I said I am going to do it so that when I become successful they will remember my name.

For example, the company may get the card, look at it and throw it in the trash, but I believe that when someone gets a card they usually tend to open up the envelope because they want to see who the card is from and they may be thinking does it have something important in it. By me sending the card my name will be on it. My goal in sending the cards was to express my gratitude for firing me and letting me go. I believe that needed to be done to release any unforgiveness, animosity or anger that I was holding so that my blessings would not be hindered.

By doing this I am releasing the bondage of carrying the getting fired root of the problem and taking it to God so that this does not keep happening and I can continue to move forward in my journey of life and press towards my success. In (Philippians 3:13-15

Brethren, I do not count myself to have apprehended, but one thing I do, forgetting those things which are behind and reaching forward to those things which are ahead, I press toward the goal for the prize of the upward call of God in Christ Jesus). Another thing that I have done with companies throughout my career is that when I have applied for a job and they send me what I call a Dear John letter "stating that they have decided not to go with me and have decided to go with someone else who is more qualified." I would go back and take a look at the companies reviews to see what other people who worked with that company had to say and reply to them by saying for example, "Thank you for your response, but unfortunately I have decided to go with another company that has a good reputation worldwide and values and appreciates their employees because I don't want to work for a company that has a lot of bad reviews."

Now the reason why I started responding to the Dear John letters (rejection letters) is because I feel that a lot of these companies are turning down hardworking and good candidates without taking into consideration how they are making people feel when they send out those types of responses. Especially when you check out their reviews and see how they treat their employees. Hence the reason why so many people get fired for invalid reasons. So I used that to my advantage to let them know that even though they went with somebody else, so did I. That strategy has worked for me and made me feel better about myself. I would recommend trying that so that you can experience how it will make you feel better about yourself too if you ever find yourself in that situation. Now the first time that I got fired from a job of course was when I was young and when you're young you just think oh well…I will just get another job and move on. However, when it starts to happen too many times throughout your adult life it's no longer oh well…but why? And, what can I do about it because I have a family to feed, bills to pay and things to do.

I started to realize that when companies fire you they don't care about you, they don't care that you have a family to feed, they don't care if you have bills to pay, they don't care about your wellbeing because you're just another number to them. Therefore, it's up to you to change your destiny and make it your greatest opportunity, Plus although they don't care. Do you know Who does? I know who really cares: it's God. In (Hebrews 13:5 - Let your conduct be without covetousness, be content with such things as you have. For He Himself has said, "I will never leave you or forsake you.")

If you have been fired don't be ashamed of yourself look at it as a new beginning in your life. I have spoken to some people who say that they have never been fired from a job and I think that is awesome for them. I do think there are some people who say they've never been fired but they really have because they are ashamed so they deny it to keep a good exterior. Now there have been many jobs that I've worked at and I wasn't fired from. I worked in different types of fields from armed security, retail stores, hotels. Those jobs weren't part of the corporate world and were good jobs, they just weren't the fields I wanted to keep working in.

The good thing about having different work

experiences is that I can always fall back on these fields if I ever needed to but for now I am now pressing forward to the things that lie ahead. It's always fun when you start a new job and one of the questions that they always ask is "Where do you see yourself in five years?" I always thought to myself that I am going to try and stay at whatever I get for at least 20 years and hopefully retire one day. Unfortunately these days it's hard to stay at the same job. Sometimes the reason is because the job isn't a good fit or because maybe it's not something that you like and other times it's because a person gets fired. There are so many reasons why people can't always expect to stay at the same job, which is another reason I decided to write this book.

Phase 2

It is January 2023 and this time last year my mother was in the hospital for COVID and a month later she passed away. I am an Ordained Minister and I do speak at funerals and prepare eulogies for funerals. I ended up doing 3 funerals back to back that year which included doing my own mothers funeral. Then after that during the year 2022 me and my wife were supposed to go on a trip to Mexico and something came up so we had to postpone it. Close to the end of 2022 my vehicle broke down and I had to get another one. The things that I just mentioned are reasons why getting fired from a job can be so devastating like at the beginning of 2023 when I got fired from my job. I bring this up because sometimes people think that just because you go to church and dress real nice and serve the Lord you don't have any problems. I am here to tell you that you're wrong and in (Psalms 34:19 - Many are the afflictions of the righteous, But the Lord delivers them out of them all). It's time to bounce back and not expect anybody to give me a pity party, a pity party does not pay any bills or solve any problems. It was time to make a move and prove to myself that I could hold myself accountable for the choices that I made and currently make.

I have spoken these words to myself repeatedly for encouragement, I will, I can, and I must execute my success to be successful. Nothing can stop me or hold me back except if I get in my own way. Alright now the testing is really coming on, we are still in January and this morning my wife needed to leave in her own car but it would not start. Then I tried to jump the vehicle with mine and my vehicle would not start, and I also had to leave. So I went to the auto store to purchase a battery starter and it stated that I had to wait 24 hrs to 36 hrs to get a charge. The next day my wife was able to leave but mine did not start. I called my insurance to have someone come and give me a jump start. I spoke to the guy and he mentioned that it might be the battery, he stated that we can try that and he could bring and install one for me. I told him to let's do that and give it a try. The tow truck driver arrived and came to find out that was the problem.

The interesting thing about this situation is that when the tow truck guy came he started talking about all that he has been going through in his life and that last year he lost a girlfriend in a car crash and that when he was going to church, he kind of fell back and was wondering what God wanted him to do. After he finished up he was still talking and then started to tear up. I gave him a hug because he really was hurting. I then ministered to him and prayed for him. We exchanged numbers and I told him to call me if he ever needed prayer or to talk.

I will say that you never know how, what, when God will send someone your way that you will have to pray with or pray for, what I do know is that this truly is a testing phase that is only temporary of where God is taking me. I have decided to apply for some different types of jobs that I was interested in working for. In life we have to decide that we cannot allow ourselves to be failures and understand that failing is not an option, it's a choice. The storm has to happen in our lives in order for the sun to shine and for you to see a breakthrough. There will be people around you that do not want to see you succeed or don't want the best for you. There may be times when you feel alone or that you may have to do things by yourself. Some people like to take advantage of people when they are down and treat them badly instead of being supportive and lifting them up.

At some point everybody needs help and you cannot help those who don't appreciate the help that you give them. If you have gotten fired from a job don't let that job break your spirit, you have to realize that you are somebody and that when one door closes another one will open. In (Hebrews 11:1 - Now faith is the substance of things hoped for, the evidence of things not seen.) (2 Corinthians 5:7 For we walk by faith, not by sight.)

Phase 3

Alright, it is now January 27th 2023 and God is moving. I heard back from 3 jobs that I applied for and have 2 interviews next week. This morning I participated in the morning prayer and that went great Praise the Lord! I want to tell everyone who purchased and is reading this book that I appreciate and thank you. I hope that as I go through this journey this will help and encourage someone else and they can be blessed. This is a test that I am going through so continue reading because I will say that things can only get better.

In (James 1:2-4 My brethren, count it all joy when you fall into various trials, knowing that the testing of your faith produces patience. But let patience have his perfect work, that you may be perfect and complete, lacking nothing). Which means that when our faith is tested, then our character will grow. I will mention that if you have been fired from a job or even left a job and you still have an old t-shirt, coffee cup, mugs, hats, anything from a company that you are no longer at. Don't live in the past, move forward to the new beginnings in your life and not ponder over what should and could have been. Don't be that person that when you go out to gatherings and you wear a shirt or a hat from a job with the company logo to make yourself look good and people like to see and assume that you still work there, who cares get rid of it and wear something else. Don't feel embarrassed, like a loser and that your world just stopped. When you lose a job you will feel like questioning yourself like "Who am I without a job?"

Don't let yourself start to have all these feelings that make you start feeling traumatic, anxiety and depression, losing your self-confidence and self-esteem. Feeling this way can make you feel shame, worthlessness which is common for most people. Sometimes this can take years for someone to recover from getting fired from a job. But I am here to tell you in (Philippians 4:13 - I can do all things through Christ who strengthens me). In (Psalms 118:17-19 - I shall not die, but live, and declare the works of the Lord. The Lord has chastened me severely, But He has not given me over to death. Open to me the gates of righteousness, I will go through them, and I will praise the Lord). Martin Luther King Jr said it best. If you can't fly then run, if you can't run then walk, if you can't walk then crawl. But whatever you do, you have to keep moving forward.

Now while going through this journey, I also realized that my wife says, "That God is going to bless me because I am not just thinking of myself, but thinking of the bigger picture by looking out for my family who is looking up to me to provide and protect them."

In (Proverbs 18:22 - He who finds a wife, finds a good thing and obtains favor from the LORD). I have given it some thought to really analyze my situation and noticed that all the jobs that I have been fired from were in the same geological location like Centennial, Englewood which is a very popular location for

Corporate Businesses. When I worked in the heart of Denver, Downtown, Aurora I never had any issues. But I am also not saying that this applies to everybody because your experiences could be the opposite or never had these types of discoveries from your job journeys. But moving forward my plan is to make sure that I do not do the exact same thing and apply for jobs in those areas. It's just like saying that if you keep doing the same thing over and over and expecting different results it becomes insanity. At this time I am going to provide different issues from only a couple of jobs so that you can see what my journey has been from these jobs. There may be some people who may have experienced these types of issues all across the states. But I just want to put it out there that if you are then you're definitely not alone and to keep reminding yourself that I am somebody and things will get better.

Jobs

Now the companies that I will mention will be prescribed as JOB1, JOB2, JOB3, JOB4 and also I will substitute names of people as Employee, Supervisor, Manager, Assistant Supervisor. I will only give these examples so that people can get the point. Now when I started for JOB1 I did Customer Service work and this was a company that was well known for their dispatch service. I would help people by troubleshooting their phones when they were having connection issues. At that time this was a good job with great benefits. But one thing that I will say is that working in this position or any Customer Service position there has always been politics when it comes to stats like metrics, (AHT) average handling time and quality.

Quality has always been very challenging because it always seemed that a person can take 100 calls and out of the 100 good they try to find something wrong to criticize and stop people from getting a good score or bonus. That was one thing that I did not like about working in the Call Center environment. I ended up staying there for 2 years and then me and my wife had decided that we wanted to live in another state because this was something that we had never done. So I applied for a position in North Carolina and got it. We set up a time when I needed to leave Colorado and move there. We loaded up our vehicle, put our stuff in storage and drove there. We ended up having to stay in a hotel for 2 weeks because the place was not ready.

Once we finally got our place we were without our furniture for 1 month. After we got settled in I had taken some time to go back and get our furniture and drive back. So now moving forward we are settled in with everything. I get to work and I am introduced to everyone. At first it always seems that people start out as being nice and friendly. Now the position that I applied for in North Carolina was still Customer Service but it was a little different. I was doing emails and making outbound contacts to customers regarding their services with JOB1. In this position I was not fully trained because they only had a limited number of people in that department. I will say with a list of 6 people including myself.

The Supervisor started out being nice but was not at all helpful when it came to asking questions. The only thing the supervisor did was have me sit with people and said that if I had any questions to ask the people who I was sitting with which at that time it was called shadowing. By this time we had been in North Carolina for about 1 year and things were going ok there with no issues. So now that we have experienced living there. We decided that we wanted to come back to Colorado. And in order for a person to get a job transfer they had to be in their position for at least 6 months. I will add that there is no wrong or right when a person or people change their minds of what they want to do with their life just as long as you are pressing forward to better yourself and making good decisions. Now since I have been at my job long enough and things are going good.

One day at work I approached my Supervisor and explained that I have decided to go back to Colorado and would like to get a job transfer and that I had already mentioned it to Human Resources and they stated that they would be glad to have me back and to speak with my Supervisor about getting transferred back to Colorado. The Supervisor was a little disappointed and said that she would get back to me. The next day when I came to work the Supervisor pulled me in the office and said that she had decided to let me go and that they were not going to provide me with any transfer. I then got my belongings and went home. Now we still left North Carolina after about a month of me getting fired. So I told my wife that when we get back I am going to go up to JOB1 and speak to Human Resources about what happened to see if I can get my job back. When we got back and got settled in. I went up to JOB1 and spoke to Human Resources about getting my job back, they stated that they needed to look into this and will reach out to me.

A week has gone by and I still have not heard from JOB1. I called and left messages, I even went back up there and they kept avoiding me. But after going through all this I decided to move on. Now when I started JOB2 this was a different type of field. Because in this field I was doing Collections and calling people for them to pay on their car loans. This was also a fun and challenging job. Their criteria was based on hitting your goal at the end of the month, dollars collected with no non-sufficient funds returns and then you get a bonus.

JOB2 I was with them for a long time and made good money with bonuses. I stayed in the same position for years and then took a promotion in the new department. My position was the Liaison Representative which I would be between the customer, repossession and the auction departments. When I started this position I was side trained and there was a lead who was responsible for checking the team's work and reporting it back to the Supervisor. So the lead had always acted as if they were in charge because they have been there for a long time. I noticed that when I worked in this department there were no guys on the team and I was the only one. At times it was uncomfortable but I still hung in there. After being here for a while there were rumors that another company was going to take over and they were going to lay off.

So now 6 months into my position I get an email from Human Resources stating that I needed to speak with them. I went down to Human Resources and was told that there was a list of people they were going to let go and my name came up. Before I met with Human Resources there was a guy who mentioned that the company was going to let people go who have been there longer than 5 years so they don't have to pay them severance or approve them for getting unemployment. So now I am in Human Resources and she told me that they have decided to let me go and to fill out a paper forcing me to resign from my position. I did not sign the paper so I was able to gather my belongings and they escorted me out.

I moved on and came to find out a year later the company closed down and was taken over by another company. I did not choose to apply for that company. But I did run into a couple of people throughout the years who said that they went to work for the other company and that almost everybody who was at JOB2 was working there.

Now JOB3 is a Brokerage company and I only worked for them for one year. The type of work that I did was answer incoming calls and provide information about the market and if customers wanted to know more about their portfolio then I would transfer the call to a trading license specialist. This criteria was different and the expectation was to provide excellent Customer Service and make sure all calls were not transferred only if the customer wanted more details about their portfolio. The training for this position was for 3 weeks and after that you would go through a shift bid. What I liked about this training was that it was informational and they did not test you, but gave a lot of information and allowed the class to listen to some of the agents' calls that were on the floor. After training I got the shift that I wanted which at the time I worked nights with weekends off and things were going well but was told that shift bids would be every 6 months unless I wanted to keep my shift. After about a year things changed. I had bid for a morning shift with weekends off. I had a new supervisor with a new team.

The problem became the Supervisor looking for issues and wanting to see me fail. The Supervisor was a new Supervisor trying to make a point that if it's not their way it is the highway. This Supervisor was not good at all; they would meet with me every day and make it seem as though I was not performing well.

After about a month with this new Supervisor I was pulled into a conference with another a second Supervisor and the new Supervisor stating that my performance was not up to par and they wanted to put me on an action plan. They provided me with a time frame and if by that time there was no improvement then they were going to have to terminate me. So when the time frame had come close I approached my new Supervisor and asked how I was doing. She told me that in order for me to speak about that. I needed to email her and set up a time for us to speak. So I went back to my desk and emailed her to ask how I am doing with my performance.

She never responded or replied and after a week went by and it was time to meet up in the conference room with the Supervisor and the second Supervisor again. I came in early that morning and got my belongings and knew this was the day that I was going to get fired and left. Even if I did not leave that day it was going to happen. I was going to be fired based on performance. But in my opinion I believe there was more to the story that's undercover because of the way it all happened if you know what I mean. I can base it on a lot of factors especially if you or someone has had these similar situations happen to them. The number one reason most companies have fired people was based on work performance as an excuse in some cases.

JOB4 I actually stepped out of my comfort zone and stopped working behind a desk and started to do a driving job. I have done driving jobs before but I thought this driving job was going to be different and challenging. With this job I would load and unload the truck that I would be going out on a route to make deliveries. Now when I started with JOB4 things were going swell for a whole year.

Then when the next year came around people started to show and act in different ways. On this particular day I was doing my job and preparing a lane that was boxed or wrapped with furniture. Then surprisingly the Supervisor approached me and asked me to go outside in the back to pick up some trash around the hill (this was not part of my job or job description). Because whenever the wind would blow, some of the trash had got scattered around the building and wanted me to clean it up. The Supervisor also stated that it was going to be nice outside and to get some sunshine. After about 15 min being outside picking up trash another employee approached me and asked me if I was on punishment. I replied to him no are you.

On a different day an Assistant Supervisor wanted me to clear out the trash on the inside of the warehouse which had broken couches, sinks, chairs, tables and crates and throw them in this big trash bin (which was not a part of my job description and no other employees were doing this). After I had gotten all of the trash in the bin the Assistant Supervisor came out and helped me with 3 little items that were left to throw in the trash. After that he had me prepare deliveries for the next day. On this day I punched in at about 6am and went to go help unload a truck. I ended up finishing at about 8 am. I went into the break room to take a break and sit down. When I came out of the break room an employee asked me if I knew what work was. I replied yes the work that you are doing on your bench I said why? The employee stated that I needed to get to work. I told him that he was not my boss and to go and kick rocks.

On this day I applied for a position that was open

and expressed my interest to the Assistant Supervisor and the Supervisor in that department. They both mentioned to me that it was great. Then the Assistant Supervisor later mentioned to me that they were not going to be hiring for that position and for me to hold off. When it was time to go home the Supervisor in the other department said that she never heard of the position being on hold and that she was going on vacation and will be back next week to see if they had scheduled any interviews. The next day I approached the Assistant Supervisor and mentioned that I thought about what he said about the hiring being put on hold and if he was just saying that because the posting came out yesterday. He said that he was not making it up and the order needed to be to talk to the Supervisor, Assistant Supervisor, and then the Supervisor in the other department. He also said that the position was going to be put on hold and held for someone else and that he did not want me to get my hopes up. He also mentioned that the Supervisor in the other department will be on vacation. The Assistant Supervisor mentioned that last week when I was working there were 2 items that did not get worked on and it was brought to his attention. I told him that I did all my work and that was not true. He said that it would be best for me to keep plugging in the position that I am in.

The Assistant Supervisor also mentioned that moving forward I am going to be used when people call in or don't show up for work in order for me to go on the truck. On this day I did not feel well and called in. On that same day the Assistant Supervisor called me back and said that I could not miss any more time, personal time. On that same day I reviewed my time and wrote it down to have a discussion about it and how it works. On this day me and the Supervisor had a conversation about my time. I told him that I spoke to the Manager about it, but he never got back to me. I also mentioned and presented to him the inaccuracy of my personal time that was used for my bereavement and bereavement for personal and some other days that should have been for vacation. The Supervisor stated that I had the highest percentage in damage deliveries and that when working there were some inconsistencies. I told him that this was the first that I have heard of this and I thought I was doing good because we never had this conversation seeing that I have been here for a whole year now. He said that some of the drivers gave him feedback. I told him that this was new to me and when I asked him about my time.

The Supervisor said that he was not worried about that and it would be a process to change it through Human Resources and that missing time once a month was too much, unless it was like every 3 months and not a pattern. After our conversation he said to get with the Assistant Supervisor. On this day I spoke to another employee in the warehouse about how personal time works. He said that they do not tell you how it works, but only if you use it too much they will speak with you. I also spoke to another employee on the same day and he said that it all starts all over at the beginning of the year. On this day I spoke with another employee about time and he said that when he started it was unlimited time for people to call in with no issues and that when he called in nobody would say anything about it. On this day I was helping unload and when I had got one of the items on a dolly this employee kept saying, "Boy."

I turned around and said, "Who are you calling, 'boy'?"

At that moment I felt like punching him, but instead I corrected him and told him to call me by my name. Then after I finished unloading The Supervisor was speaking with an employee that if you're not being a good delivery driver and you are bad then you will be stuck in the warehouse (which he was hinting to him that I am in the warehouse. I have been in the warehouse for 4 months straight which was not part of the job description). When I started with JOB4 I was told that everyone gets 2 weeks in the warehouse and 4 weeks as a driver.

Later that day I spoke to the other Supervisor in the other department about my time and she said that she coded everything correctly and then for bereavement they only give out five days, but they gave me an extra bereavement day. An employee approached me and asked me to come and see him when I got a chance because he wanted to ask me something personal. When I got over there he said that he heard the Supervisor and the Assistant Supervisor had come down on me. I told him no and that it was just about me calling in and my time. The employee stated that if there was anything else going on to let him know because he has been there for seventeen years and he has seen some stuff, I asked him if it was surrounded by race or favoritism. He said favoritism and if I had experienced race here (I told him no, that I get along with everybody here. Also, because I did not trust him like that to confide in him if that is the case).

The next day the same employee wanted to go to lunch with me out of the blue. And when we left he stated that he just wanted to confirm that I was not experiencing any race situation. I told him not just a misunderstanding of my time and that I get along with everybody. The employee also mentioned that the time is basically under the discretion of the Supervisor.

On this day an employee who was a new driver that has been here for 3 weeks came to me while I was working in the warehouse and that 2 employees were talking bad about, but he did not reveal what they were saying, but he mentioned to them that if they have a problem with me they should go and talk to me about it instead of talking behind my back. On this day I was helping unload using a dolly. And when I was walking backwards an employee tied a rope from the entrance side to side. I caught it in time before I got injured.

Now when I brought it to his attention that I could have gotten injured he started laughing and I told him that I didn't think that was funny at all. On this day an employee asked if he could change the music in the warehouse and when another employee heard that he shouted out real loud that the music was cultural you f***, who doesn't like David Bowie and when other people in the warehouse heard that they all started laughing. On this day I was approached by the Assistant Supervisor and he told me that I would be going out on the truck with the employee who made that comment in the warehouse.

The next day I went out with the employee who made that comment on the truck. We were told this day that the Supervisor and the Assistant Supervisor will be out of the office and that they put an employee in charge. The employee who I was on the truck with made a comment like he cannot wait to see the employee who is in charge to yell and tell people off. When we got back to the warehouse an employee approached me and said, "I did not see you today, they finally let you out of prison and jail."

I did not respond to his comment, but told him that my day was good. On this day I came to work and the front office door was locked and I saw people going around to the back. When I got into the warehouse I approached the employee who they said they left in charge and told him that the front office door was locked. The employee in charge said to me that the door was locked because I was let go and did I get my pink slip because I would have to work in the basement. I replied to him where my slip was. He just looked at me and walked away. I also approached the Supervisor in the other department to let her know that the front office door was locked. She said that something was wrong with her key because when she unlocks it and someone badges in it locks the door. But she stated that she was aware of the situation.

On this day I went out on the truck with another employee and when we got back to the warehouse he a made a comment that all black people that he has hung with or been around there first names always begins with a D and gave examples like Darrell who use to work here, and old friend who contacted him named Derrick, and the guy who works here with us named Dwayne and then me. I told him that I was not aware or even thought of anything like that. On this day I went out on the truck with another employee and he said that Management is looking for people to fire and my name has been brought up. I told him thanks for letting me know and that I would keep my eyes open. He then started laughing and changed the subject. On this day I had a scheduled meeting with the Supervisor to speak on my yearly talk. But when I came in I was told that I was scheduled to go out on the truck.

When I got back, I approached the Supervisor about meeting with him and he just replied yea and brushed me off and continued to talk with the Assistant Supervisor. After this day I still have not met with the Supervisor and when I asked other people if they have spoken and met with the Supervisor the majority has said yes. The same day me and another employee delivered a sleeper and I was walking backwards and when I got to the 5th step on the porch I fell sitting down and hurt my back. After we got back to the warehouse I brought it to the Assistant Supervisor about the incident and he just acted like oh well and said I hope you feel better and will see you tomorrow.

On this day I was working in the warehouse and I had to take a table over to the other department to look at and out of nowhere an employee yelled real loud across the warehouse, "What are you doing? I need you over here to unload this truck."

He said this while I was getting some assistance from another employee to fix this table. But he did not yell for anyone else to assist him like that. On this day me and another employee were removing the plastics that were in this machine that needed to be changed. The lever was hard to open and it popped out. So the employee used a rope and tied it to the lever. I helped him and when we both pulled on the rope it popped open and I fell backwards on my behind and it triggered my back hurting. I got up and was stiff and was unable to move. This was at the end of my shift when it was time to go home. I told the Supervisor in the other department about it. The next day I called the other Supervisor in the other department early in the morning and told her that I was not going to make it in because my back was hurting.

She replied, "Sorry, but we are definitely going to need you tomorrow. Please rest up."

The next day I came to work with my back still hurting. On this day in the break room there were holiday cookies and crackers and other snacks on the table for anyone to have. So on my way home I grabbed a pack of cookies to bring home to my family. The next couple of days an employee approached me early in the morning and said that another employee is going to tell the Supervisor that I had taken some cookies out of the break room and that was considered stealing and not to worry about because it's not like anyone else had gotten any from the break room and that she was just picking on me.

That same day I had gotten change for a $20 dollar bill that I had in my pocket. I then approached the employee and asked if she had any grandkids because my mom passed away and they miss their grandmother. She said that she didn't have any grandkids but had a teenager. So I gave her $5 dollars and told her Merry Christmas and that she can do whatever she wants with it. At first the employee was refusing but I told her that's ok and she said that she would put it in her church offering. On this day I went out on the truck with another employee and he was telling me that another employee was complaining about the time that me and him went out on a truck and said that I was too old and he would never want to ride on the truck with me again. The employee stated that he told the other employee that he has never had any issues and that we work fine.

On this day there was a morning meeting with the Assistant Supervisor and he mentioned that they had a new employee starting in a couple of weeks and he will permanently be assigned to a truck. I have noticed that everyone who has started after me since last year has been permanently assigned to a truck and I have been assigned as a stager for when people call out or they need an extra person on the truck. On this day after loading the trucks I asked an employee if he had a conversation with the Supervisor regarding his yearly increase yet because he has not talked with me. The employee said that he spoke to him last week and that it doesn't matter if you do good or bad, it's all going to be the same across the board. I also asked another employee if he had spoken with the Supervisor about the yearly increase. He said that he also spoke to him last week as well. I told him that he has not talked with me about it and the employee responded that I probably was not going to get one and laughed about it.

Last week up until now everyone has spoken to the Supervisor about their yearly that he has pulled into his office or that he has approached. The Supervisor has been ignoring me whenever he sees me and continues to have conversations with other employees and acts as though I am not around. A couple days later as I was working in the warehouse the Assistant Supervisor came to me and said that we needed to meet in the Supervisors office. As we sat in the office the Supervisor stated that there have been more issues with my performance and after he has spoken with other drivers then they have decided to terminate my employment. Now that you have read what I have been through with my jobs. I don't expect my situation to be mirrored or people to think that their experiences have not been important because they have been through a lot. I feel that this is the time to embrace who we are and continue to stay lifted up.

Now I am not a perfect man but very humble. I have made mistakes in my life just like the next person and I don't believe in being judgmental because we can all be one paycheck from being homeless. But I pray that nobody will get one paycheck from being homeless. (Psalms 37: 25 - I have been young and now am old, yet I have not seen the righteous forsaken, nor his descendants begging bread). In (Proverbs 18:21 - Death and life are in the power of the tongue, and those who love it will eat its fruit). In (Psalms 118: 17 -24 - I shall not die, but live, and declare the works of the LORD, The LORD has chastened me severely, But He has not given me over to death. Open to me the gates of righteousness; I will go through them, and I will praise the LORD).

I remember how great I used to feel when starting a job and people would get real proper training. Most training that was good for me are the ones that were 2 weeks, 3 weeks, and even 5 weeks. And when you were finished with training they would only let you go if you felt comfortable being on your own to work by yourself whether it was in a Call Center, Retail,

Security. Now I have noticed that most jobs have shortened their training by allowing people to do more shadowing and providing only 1 week of training in some industries. To me training plays a big part in a person either being set up to fail or succeed depending on who is teaching you. I have always taken the approach to self-teach myself and be proactive and not depend on instructors and teachers for certain things in training. We want to believe that when someone is standing in front of you that they know what they are talking about. Sometimes they do if they have studied their craft and not just there to get a paycheck and really want people to succeed.

Make sure when you are in a training setting ask a lot of questions if you don't know and are not sure. Pick their brain and step outside the box. Really research and learn about the position, google and look at reviews from people who are or were in the position to see if it will be a good fit for you. Check out the credentials of a trainer or instructor and see if they have a good rapport and success rate. Don't settle or become desperate. Look for signs that give off red flags when you're in training. There are so many jobs out there that are really good and not saying that the one you have won't be good. But just be careful because I am. And first and foremost, pray about it and see what God has to say and if it becomes confirmed.

UPDATE: Remember when I mentioned that I had 3 Interviews. Well, I went to all three and accepted one. The one that I accepted is a company that is going to pay for me to get a CDL. I started February 20th and went to a pre-class training that was to prepare people to take the test at the DMV. As I was getting prepared and taking in-class tests and notes. I was told that after three days of class I would have to go down and take the test and come back next Monday when I pass to start the next part of training. The test consisted of general knowledge, passenger, and air brakes. When I took the test I passed the general knowledge and passenger but failed twice on the air brakes. DMV will only allow people to take the test twice a day if they fail. So that same day I came back home and studied the air brakes section again.

The next day early in the morning I went to take the test and passed. God is good, now I am ready to move to the next level. Once I passed the test I had to get back in line to take my picture. They provided me with a CDL paper permit which I also received in the mail. When next week came I was introduced to three instructors. In the training class the instructor who was going to be teaching the class wanted to get a copy of my CDL permit and Driver's License. After getting a copy in class we were told that we had to take a 350 question test once we complete 9 days of in class training. Then after that we will be learning how to drive and maneuver a different type of truck which is called (BTW) behind the wheel.

During the training we were told that you can only have one license and that when we get our CDL you have to hand in your Driver's License. What also was mentioned is that having a CDL you are held at a higher standard and there are only eight points instead of twelve, because with a Driver's License you have twelve.

In the same week of training, we had different people come in to talk with us and speak of how they like their job, how long they have been with the company and what they like about the company. After hearing and meeting people, Supervisors, Managers come to find out the employees are protected by the union and Management and Supervisors are not. A union representative came in to speak with us and explained that Colorado is an "at will" Employment state, which means that an employer can fire you for almost any petty reason (so long as it is not one of the few areas protected by discrimination laws).

By contrast, most union contracts protect you from being disciplined or fired for no good reason. Instead, you may only be punished for just cause. An employer must prove each and every element of just cause, or the union can win your job back, with back pay. The reason a person would need to be represented is because if you feel you have been treated unfairly, Management has not followed procedures and a difference arises between yourself and a Manager or Supervisor, you have the right to due process, that is, hearings to address your side of the story, and to a full and fair investigation of all circumstances. In essence a representative works to protect the rights of member employees.

------------------------ ❧ ------------------------

Phase 4

UPDATE: God is Good! So while going through training BTW (Behind The Wheel) I have learned how to operate and drive a bus and the safety that goes along with it. During my training I had to learn how to back up and do parallel parking and going through cones. Once that was accomplished then there were three instructors that showed you how to do and operate driving and doing things differently. I also had to learn the pre-trip part of the test. Pre-trip is learning some of the emergency and engine compartments in case of failure and when checking to make sure the bus is safe that if something goes wrong a person can identify what the problem is, not that a person has to be a mechanic but to be familiar with what would need to be fixed.

So there are 3 tests that have to be taken. 1) Pre-trip 2) Maneuvering through cones and backing up 3) Driving test. I took my test on April 18th and passed the first 2 tests. But I failed on the driving because of a train track that I forgot to signal to the right lane. One thing about taking the CDL test is that it is not like the DMV test. When you fail one you have to take the whole thing over even if you passed the other two. I spoke to an instructor about how when you fail you should just have to take that one test that a person failed on. The instructor said that they used to have it that way but in the future they are thinking of changing that back. So now I had to reschedule to take the test all over again the same week.

On April 20th I had taken the test all over and passed the second time Praise the Lord!! Now this was a long journey and I kept pressing through. There were times I did feel like giving up, but I didn't. This shows you that whatever a person wants to do you can be successful doing it without giving up. Hard work pays off and if you stay diligent you can too make a better life for you and your family. I surprised my wife and family when I came home that day that I passed my CDL and they were proud of me. The co-workers that I worked with gave me a congratulations card and had all signed it. I thought that was cool and I will make sure to pay it forward and celebrate others for their success.

One thing I have realized is that when you help others and God sees that then he will help you, because it shows that you don't have to be selfish and just worry about yourself. So if what you are going through right now during your storm reach out to others and take some time to celebrate and encourage or see how you can help someone. For example, I will tell this brief story. The beginning of this week April 17th after I got off work I had to take my son to a couple of places and when we got home I could not open my trunk. Come to find out he left his jacket in the back and it got caught in the hatch and I was unable to open it. So I tried to pry it out, press the door from the inside and it just would not budge.

So he said, "Dad you can burn it and it will get loose."

I told him that it would cause more damage. So I

made a deal with him because it was a nice jacket. I had to cut the jacket loose and told him I would buy him another one or whatever he wanted. He wanted to go to O'Reilly's auto zone to get a tool, which is what he wanted. So we drove to O'Reilly's and he got his tool. When we came back home I cut the jacket and was still unable to get the jacket out. After several hours I noticed that it was really stuck. I then looked on you tube and the owner's manual to see if there was an emergency latch, but there was neither. I called the dealership and they said that it was going to cost $695 to remove the truck and I would have to leave the vehicle with them for a couple of days.

After that I said, "I will keep trying to get it out every day that I get off work."

It is now April 24th and I am off. I got up early in the morning to work on getting some of the ripped pieces off. Now I did get some of the pieces off and told my son that we can see if we can burn some of the pieces that were stuck. I used his suggestion and burned a little bit and then pressed the trunk open with my feet and it popped open. I thanked him and told him that he was a blessing and that I needed to go get all this vacuumed up. He rode with me and helped vacuum the whole vehicle. It is the little things that can make a difference when you help somebody. Sometimes it does not have to be something really big. But when you do get help or you help somebody be appreciative and thankful because you never know when you will really need help. Ok now back to some more work.

After getting out of revenue which is the other part of training when an instructor rides with you when you are going on route for a week before you drive on your own. So when I finished I found out that everyone has to do a shift bid and it is based on seniority. I was way last to pick my shift and the way it looks people who have been here for a while of course they get straight shifts and weekends off. But the ones who were low on the totem pole like myself got split shifts and had to work weekends. Now after selecting my shift, I was still able to go to church but the way it was set up I had to meet my wife at church and when church let out I had to go back to work to do my second part of my shift. They stated that the shift bids are done every 4 months and on top of that the company is short of people so they said that people have to pick one of these days of to work whatever hours and if you did not set your shift up they will pick a shift for you to work and it has to be done every week. So now I only have one day off while working this job that is in demand. Even people who have been here for a long time are also mandated to do the same thing. I have run into people who have been here for 10, 17, 20, 25 years.

On May 24th I was driving downtown and there was a shuttle bus dropping off some passengers and the bus was on the right and I was in the middle lane. So as I was passing the shuttle bus my mirror and the other bus touched mirrors and there was no damage, nothing broken, no scratches, not cracked. And the driver called it in and the dispatch called me while I was driving and asked if my mirror was damaged. I told him no and I kept driving. As I was continuing my route I was not told to pull over or anything by dispatch and in about 5 min later a Supervisor from another division stopped and got out of the vehicle and was taking pictures and said there was no damage and that my Supervisor from my department will have me fill out an incident report. And to make sure if something is hit to stop the bus and pull over. Then 10 minutes later one of the Supervisors showed up and I filled out an incident report about what happened. It was brought to my attention that if there is any accident, anything that hits the bus even if there is no damage and it's not your fault to pull the bus over and notify dispatch and wait for a Supervisor to come to me. I was like oh boy I could not believe that it just barely grazed the mirror and there was no damage to the other shuttle bus either.

Now I work a shift where I have to get up pretty early to start my day. Sometimes 3:30 am, 4:00 am, or even 4:30 am. I enjoy the job but now I have to make sure there is balance for life and family time. The interesting thing is that I have not been in church since my schedule changed and I now work on Sundays. I will continue to attend church since my schedule changed and will have to leave right after and go back to work. Well with that being said this week I am taking my wife on a date so that we can continue to live our life even though I work early hours. Alright so now the shift bid.

When I bid for my shift I was the lowest one at number 138 out of 230 people. So the way that it works is for example Sunday would be from 4:11 am-9:35 am route 6 then from 1:39 pm to 4:46 pm route 76 then off work. Monday, Tuesday, Wednesday, 4:46 am- 1040 am route 51 then from 11:43 am to 3:03 pm. And also come to find out that the company was short 25 drivers so they mentioned that people will have to work one of their off days and if they did not pick a shift voluntarily then a shift will be picked for you to work and I was off Thursday and Friday so I picked Thursday to work if it was available if not then I would pick a shift for Friday. Come to find out everybody plus the people who have been here for ten plus years have to work the mandated overtime. I am getting to the point where I might have to look somewhere else but not no time soon because me and my wife have our 31-year anniversary coming up and also our trip to Hawaii.

After I get through that I will start looking for a job that has work, life, balance. I was told by other employees that they have been mandating overtime before the pandemic and that the job is not for everybody because they have a high turnover rate and most people are not use to doing split shifts which I definitely understand, unless you are single and just want to work and don't have a life, family to spend time with then this job is for you. It is a job that is really in demand and seems as though all they care about is getting shifts covered and not worrying about people getting burnt out.

One day I came in from my morning route and my manager said that she needed to talk with me. I did not think I was any kind of trouble but you never know. So I went into her office and she started asking me what type of job I did before I came here. I told her I was a delivery driver and been driving for a couple of years and got out of the corporate world of sitting behind a desk. She said that is what I wanted to talk to you about. Your name came up during a conversation and asked how I would like to apply for their Supervisor position because she thinks I would be great at it. She went on to explain the duties that came along with it.

Like doing incident reports, going on routes, working dispatch, if people call to find replacements. She also stated that they had 15 Supervisors and they also had to do a bid based on seniority. She said if I was interested to give it some thought and think about it.

After that I left her office and one thing that I thought about is that if I did take that position I would be in a worse situation than I am now. I might have to work graveyards, have a worst shift because I would still be that last man on the list. Also, when you're a Supervisor you are not in the union and do not have to pay union fees. I would not feel that there would be job protection especially after getting fired from jobs why would I want to go backwards. There used to be a time in life and my career that I wanted to move up in the company and be a Supervisor, but at this time in my life I just want to work smarter not harder and have a life balance to spend time with my family and travel. When I work the splits after completing a route they have a pool table that people can play while waiting for their next route to start. I am not a pool player but I tried it and it was fun when there was enough time to play. After meeting with my Supervisor, I decided to ask other people if they were interested in being a Supervisor because I did not want to do that either. Most people who I approached declined and said they would make more money driving.

So the next day I gave it some thought and told my Manager that I was not interested and she replied that she thought that she would ask and did not want to force me to do anything that I would not wanna do. So I thanked her and moved on. Then that same day 4 Supervisors approached me and were trying to convince me to apply and that it would be a good move. I told them all that I was not interested at this time so they accepted it and moved on. Now here is something important that I wanted to share before I continue.

On May 12 I had an appointment with the dealership to get an oil change, alignment and to check this 4 wheel drive light. The service agent said that he would contact me once everything is done. The next 2 days it was not done and I have not heard from anybody, So I initiated a call and spoke to another service agent and the person who was handling my vehicle had called in sick and said that I would have to wait until Monday. So during this time, I had to drive my wife's vehicle. Thank God we had 2 vehicles.

Now Monday comes and they still have not worked on my vehicle but said that since I have a warranty they will call to see if they will cover the transfer case and the right strut that was damaged and they would call me back. So the whole week went by and now it's Thursday May 18th and I have not heard anything. So I called the dealership again and spoke with someone else and he said that they were waiting for the warranty inspector to come and investigate the vehicle and it can take 24 to 48 hrs. So the warranty investigator comes out on Saturday and I still have not been notified after that.

Another week goes by and I ended up calling on May 22 and this time when I called I got hung up on. So since I was on my split I decided to go up there real quick to see what was going on and at this time I am heated and ready to get my vehicle and speak to the Manager. After my first route I drove up to the dealership. Once I got there I asked to speak to a Manager. Then one of the service representatives said that the reason that it was taking so long is because they were short of technicians and people were calling in sick. So I told him I understand that, but what I did not understand is that my vehicle has been here since the 12th and I have not heard from anyone. The service representative said well that if I wanted to take my vehicle I could. I told him that I want fixed for what I came in here for. Then the person who I was dealing with in the first place said that he apologized and that he was waiting to get approval from the warranty company and that the person who was supposed to work on my vehicle had a family emergency and a death in the family and if I could bring my vehicle back next week.

At this point I was livid. I told him no and that I want my vehicle fixed just like the next person and that I got hung up on, nobody has called to give an update and when is it going to be fixed and done because you're still getting paid from me and the warranty company. The service representative assured that this Wednesday coming up that it will be fixed. Now at this point I had to go and get a rental for the warranty to cover since my vehicle was getting fixed. This situation was a very terrible experience that I had ever gone through and I will not recommend or take my vehicle back to that place ever. So now when Wednesday comes and I get to pick up my vehicle I notice that when I drive on the highway it starts pulling as if they did not do the alignment, I had to call up there to bring it back in for the alignment to get correctly done and the next appointment was not until June 1st.

I went to the dealership that day and it was completely done and there were no more issues after that.

On June 27th I was approached by my Supervisor's boss and she said that she wanted to have a conversation with me real quick. I went into her office and she asked me how I felt about being a Supervisor. I told her that at this time it will not work because I am a minister and need to have Sundays off and cannot work late nights. I also told her that I have a wife. She stated that she was looking for a Supervisor that has heart and that my name came up in a conversation. I told her thanks but not at this time. Now there is a Supervisor that is in control of scheduling and he is very motivated to fill the shifts that are not filled and if people do not voluntarily select a shift to work on one of their off days they will be mandated. I will continue to work here until my next shift bid and look forward to seeing what will be available for either to stay past August or find another job.

Phase 5

Update: On July 18th there was an Interim bid that was available on the screen when you walk through the door. So I placed the bid for the shift and it closed July 21st. On July 25th it was announced that I was awarded that bid and that it will not go into effect August 13th which is perfect because me and my wife are going to Hawaii from August 7th to August 11th the shift that was available is Monday-Friday from 4:20 am to 12:31 pm with Saturday and Sundays off. However, I would still be mandated if I do not select one of my off days to work. This shift is only going to be temporary because I still will have to bid for another shift for later that will take effect on September 1st or the 10th. But the good thing is that I will have Sundays off and the goal is to get a shift that will work for me.

I told my wife that if my next shift bid does not work and has me trying to work on Sundays I definitely will be looking elsewhere. I really like this job but again if there is no balance for life I will have to move on. Now this year has been a challenge that I will say. So Saturday will be my last day working the old schedule. The Bid came out for people to see and it shows the time and seniority list. I jumped up quite high, I went from 138 to 118 which is I guess still good. When I return from vacation people will be assigned to bid from August 15th to August 18th with different time slots. I was told that you only get 5 min to select your bid. A couple of days ago I was speaking to a guy who just started and he said that he was not covered under the union yet but they are taking out money. I thought that was kind of weird. So there was a union representative that was close by from where we were sitting and I asked him about people being covered under the union.

He said, "That when a person starts earning, which means that they are on the road by themselves they are on a probationary period for 90 days. When the 90 days are up they will be permanently in the union."

Which was never told to me in the beginning. But for me that was good because August 2 I reached my 90-day mark. I will mention that being on the road I have seen some interesting people get on the bus. There was this guy who was sitting in a wheelchair and when I would pull up to let him in he would get out of his wheelchair and wait for the ramp to get on the bus. He would always get on my route every day and always ask me if I was going to 44th and Harlan.

I would say, "Yes."

And when we would arrive at his destination he would say, "See you later operator."

And then I would say, "After a while crocodile."

Which I thought was pretty cool. Then there was another guy that I would pick up and you can tell he had a problem but I do not judge people I just treat everyone fairly and then pray for them to myself. He would get on the bus with a psychology book and stand in front of me and pause and say, "Hi."

And would not move until I responded back to say hi.

Phase 6

Now I am going to just back up a little bit to cover what has been going on in July that I have been meaning to address to bring us up to date. July 4th was fun this time around. We decided to just get fireworks and drive close to the library to see the fireworks show. However, for the past 15 years we would go to see the Thornton fireworks and set up our tent that was our spot. But because of my schedule we could not go this year but it worked out. We will definitely go next year to keep our tradition going.

On July 7th I had to attend my uncle's girlfriend's funeral. He has been with for 22 years and they were never married but they loved each other. It was a different and beautiful going away celebration. They did it differently from the traditional way. They had the funeral in the mountains outside but the body was not there because they chose to cremate. Also, what was also beautiful is that at the end of the service they passed around a folded small envelope and told people not to smash or squeeze it. When it was time to open the envelope we opened it up and a butterfly flew out of it. I thought to myself that this was very different, thoughtful and nice.

Then on July 11th my cousin got killed and they found his body somewhere on a walk trail. No new information has been updated about the situation. But also, in July me and my wife went and did an overnight stay in the mountains for our anniversary. It was beautiful and we took really good pictures. Now that I was able to catch up I am through with July. The funeral for my cousin that got killed is going to be Saturday August 5th after I get off work. OH NO! I just got a call on August 3 that my other cousin was found dead from an overdose and my phone has been blowing up. Me and the wife just had a little dispute, but we were able to bring it back in because we are going on our trip in a couple of days.

Hold up I am going to stop right now and say a prayer, "Dear Heavenly Father, I pray for our family and ask that you comfort them in the time of need, forgive us our sins, LORD we need your help. I pray for a hedge of protection from the wiles of the enemy, I pray for your guidance, your safety, your traveling mercies. Thank you for your Son Jesus Christ for dying on the cross and shedding his blood to wash away our sins. I pray that my prayers are answered in Jesus' name Amen. Anytime you go through something always pray, pray without ceasing. Praying will get you through whatever situations you are going through. Don't give up just because you're hurting. We all hurt in some kind of way. Be strong and grow closer to God he will never leave you or forsake you. You got this and so do I. We are going to make it through this year no matter what."

UPDATE: So we made it back from Hawaii and let me tell you how it went. When we first landed there it looked like a plain run-down city from the 70's look. We thought that we were going to see a tropical island but that was not the case. I rented a car so that we could drive around and explore and drove to the hotel that we were going to be staying at. When we got there they had us booked right next to the elevator, but we ended up changing our room. The hotel was nice and there was a lot to do there so we decided to change clothes and get comfortable and go to the lower level to get something to eat. At the restaurant we ordered light because we were not that hungry since we ate earlier that day but we did have some pina coladas and they were way better from when we tried them in Colorado.

The plane was a 7-hour flight and we enjoyed that because we were able to watch movies on our phone. United used to have the screens in the back of the chairs but they do not do that anymore. People can either use a tablet or cell phone. Parking was across the street and I parked in the garage. But the next day when we left to drive around I had to park in the overflow parking that was 2 min away from the hotel. The hotel was also across the street from the beach so we did go over to the beach to get in the water and the ocean was beautiful, the waves were coming to shore with the wind blowing and it was also humid and crowded with a lot of people They did have tropical trees but we did not see any coconuts on trees, only some bananas which was interesting. The places that I drove to were the Pearl Harbor location, Pearl city, Northshore, and Turtle Bay Resort.

The places were ok but just ran down and were very expensive. It would not be a place that I would want to stay but just visit. After exploring and driving around we came back to the hotel to relax. And when I turned on the news it was saying that Maui was on fire and the whole island was burning. They said that the landmarks that were there for years got burned down and that there were 60 people who they had found not alive. Maui was burning real bad because people who were residents there had their houses burned down. That was sad and they were turning away tourists and telling everyone to evacuate. I was shocked because at first we thought about going there, but it's a good thing we didn't. When it was time to leave we took some pictures and got some souvenirs. I noticed that there were a lot of Japanese there and not so many Simoleons. Now back to work I finally got through this week and did my bid which is ok. But I did get Sunday, Mondays off, however I still will have to schedule myself for one of my off days since it is still mandated.

After getting back I received a call from a job that I applied for in the beginning of August just in case I decided to move on. I called the company back and set up an interview not thinking that things would move forward. On August 16th I had the interview and it lasted for about 2 hrs and I have never had an interview go that long. They really enjoyed my resume and work history and decided to set me up for a second interview. When I finished up I was so excited and felt like a burden was lifted off my shoulders. On my drive home I had time to think about my plans of moving forward from my current job. The thing that kept bothering me and replaying in my mind was working mandates on my off day, and if I don't schedule myself then they will schedule it for me. I realized that I would be working 6 days a week with one off day with no work, life and balance.

On August 22 I got a call to go to the second interview. When I arrived I met with a man named Bill and we talked about the job and what I would be doing and that training will be for 2 weeks. The location only takes about 15 to 20 min to get there. Bill explained that since I have my CDL that I would be driving by myself and will be loading and unloading a truck and that steel toe boots are required. When we finished talking he provided me with a paper to take a drug test and gave me his card and shook my hand and said that he looks forward to working with me. We also set up a start date which will be September 5th. After I left I went straight to take the drug test at Concentra. When I got home I decided to type up a letter of resignation and that my last day of employment will be August 29th.

The next day I went to work and after I got off I gave my letter to Human Resources and spoke to a guy named Jed. He was disappointed and asked if I wanted to speak with Kim, the Human Resource Manager, about why I was leaving. I told him no, that my decision was made and that I really liked working here because the people and the job were great but I could not deal with being mandated on my off day. I mentioned that if it was not for that I would have probably stayed, but it does not work for my life. Jed accepted the paper and said thank you. I told him that I would return my uniform on my last day of work.

On August 30th after work I went back to Human Resources to return my Items to Jed and was hoping that I did not run into anybody because I just wanted to move on and not feel bad about letting people know that I no longer work there anymore, but it was just so happen that when I pulled up to park and get out of the car, I did run into somebody and it was one of the instructors who was Danny, he was like so your leaving I told him yes I was and if it was not for the mandates I would have still been here. He said that he understood and that you have to do what you have to do. But he was the only one that I ran into and then I left.

Phase 7

Well today is September 5th and I start my new job. I felt relieved from working at the other job because it was in demand and I can admit that this time I left and it was not because they were going to let me go or get fired. Like I said before, if things would have been different I may have stayed. Moving on, so I arrived at the building that I will be working at and met the people that I will be working with.

After that I went into the manager's office with Bill and he had me fill out a whole lot of DOT paperwork which is information that deals with any accidents, drug policies, background and of course the last seven years of employment. Bill mentioned that safety is first. I told him that I am definitely aware of that since my last job. After filling out all the paperwork, Bill took me on a tour of the building and also provided me with my time number so that I could punch in and out. He then explained that the company has been around for 40 years. and he has been in the business for 50 years.

After that he went back to his office and told me that the benefits would not start until I am there for 60 days. My training will be for 2 weeks and I will be riding with someone during training to see how things flow there. My schedule will be Monday thru Friday with Saturday and Sundays off, but on the 3rd Saturday everybody works a half day shift which is a much better schedule than my previous employer. Hours will be in the morning starting at 6 am until done. Bill stated that they will provide me with a company phone with Bluetooth capabilities and if I happen to lose the phone it will cost me $300 dollars to replace it. After that I was given a hat, gloves, safety vest and he mentioned that I would need to get some steel toe boots. The day was short so after finishing up with everything he said that I could go home and that I was official and he is glad to be working with me and will see me tomorrow.

So I started the next day and was introduced to the people who were not there including the trainer who I will be riding with. My job primary duties and responsibilities will be 1) Perform complete pre and post trip inspection of the truck. 2) Safely operate the assigned truck, follow work order instructions to include specific time requests, notes, call on way instructions, and designated disposal instructions. 3) Complete required work order progression, document photos, and other route productivity information. 4) Continuously monitor the condition of the truck and containers to ensure proper maintenance of the assets. 5) Actively participating in passing customers leads to management for follow up. 6) Exhibits a sense of pride in their work and "Rides for the Brand." 7) Compliance with all Federal, State, and DOT Hours of Service procedures. My first week of training I did a ride along and learned how to do the controls on the truck. I also learned how different it was driving the truck and sitting up high.

During the third day me and the trainer started to get to know each other and the only thing that I did not like was every time he was driving down the street he would look at that lady or that woman. I was kinda avoiding his gestures, but after he kept on, I had to let him know that I was a happily married man and a minister. I showed him pictures of my wife and my minister's license. I explained to him that I am held to a higher standard and try to avoid temptation but that I am not blind and I do see but I quickly turn away from lusting and sin. I asked him about his marriage and did he have an open relationship because he always keeps turning his head and looking at other women.

Now he told me that he did not have an open relationship and that he likes what he sees. He stated that he has been married for 23 years. and has 2 children from his wife. I asked him if his wife saw what he was doing and would she be happy with him doing that. He said no and that he was trying. I told him that I would keep praying for him. The trainer told me that he and his wife was from Mexico and that one of the reasons why some of his people cross the border is because there was too much killing in his country and everybody was just wanting to better their lives, but when you have bad people trying to stop you from doing good, they either try to kill you or your family from succeeding. I told him that I had no clue about that and always that when people crossed the border it was because they could get away with it and come to the United States for free.

Now in the second week of training the trainer told me that he and his wife go to church and they are Catholics and will be taking turns with other couples hosting a Bible group. I told him that was good and to make sure he is doing that with good intentions. After finishing my 2 weeks training I was told by the manager that I would be on my own. Now when I got home my wife said that when she was leaving she accidentally backed up and hit the garage door because she got distracted by the check engine light coming on and staying on. The garage door was cracked on the bottom, but it works coming up but when going down it lifts back up. So now we have to figure out how to fix that before it gets any worse. Now the good news that I will share is that last week we got some tickets to go see the Denver Broncos vs Kansas City in November. We got some tickets a while ago to go see the Denver Broncos vs New York Jets, but came to find out Aaron Rodgers got hurt so we won't have a chance to see him play against Russell Wilson. Another thing that is good is the Colorado Buffs are doing good with Deon Sanders being the coach. The Colorado Buffs played against Colorado State and beat them 43- 35, now that was a good game. Come to find out both coaches are African American which is first in history for them to play against each other in Colorado for College. So I started my first day and came to find out the truck was having problems with the injectors so they had to put it in the shop.

Now the next couple of days I will be back with the trainer. After I finished the day I decided to go to the store and get myself a new backpack, some sanitizer, and antibacterial wipes so that when it is time for me to drive alone I will be able to clean the inside of the truck for germs. I also invested in a respiratory gas mask with filters that came with safety goggles to help from breathing in bad pollution. Remember when I said earlier that I was going to get my thank you cards to mail out to my ex-employees. I have decided to get a pack to mail them out this week. Now is the time I am going to look up the company's addresses and send out eight envelopes. I will keep you updated if I get a response or not but stay tuned.

I feel excited about it. Now during the week, the trainer let me drive and let me do things on my own as if I was doing it myself. As he was guiding me I noticed a couple of things that he was not paying attention to, like whenever I would back up he was not there making sure I did not hit anything. They did not have backup cameras or a rearview mirror for me to look at. And when it was time for him to show me how to use the controls he was like you have to use common sense and do it like this. Now I did not like his response so when we got back into the truck I had to check him and let him know that I know how to use common sense and that it's easy for him to say that because he had been doing this job for 20 years, while this was only my second time doing this. Then he was like yea that is true and you are smart, I told him I know that I am smart and then he started to be a little more patient about everything. So I drove and did everything for 2 days.

It is now September 21st and this day was Thursday and I did not drive this day the trainer did. In the morning we had a quick meeting and one of the employees asked about PTO and vacation time because when he was off he did not get paid for it and since he has been working there for a year and it has never shown up on his check. Bill explained that by the state you accumulate 1 hour for every 30 hrs worked. So one of the other employees said that he has been there for 15 years and did not know that we had time and if the time was grandfathered in. The question was not answered and pretty much everybody was kind of puzzled about not being told about time off. The trainer said that he has been there for 20 years and did not know anything about time off as well. But later that day we received a call from the Manager Bill and he asked the trainer if I was going to be ready to roll tomorrow because one of the drivers had got injured and a door hit his head and he started bleeding real bad and had to be rushed to the hospital. He told Bill that I would be ready for tomorrow instead of next week.

Now last week my wife made plans for us to go on a date and that this Friday after work I would need to make sure that I was off by 5 pm. I made sure that I mentioned it to the trainer about making sure that I am off by 5 pm on Friday and that I will let the Supervisor know when we get back. We finished up for the day and the Supervisor was back at the office to let me know that I would be by myself and have 5 stops to do. I explained to him that it would be fine but needed to be done by 5 pm. He stated that it all depends on me, that I could be finished by 1:30 pm or 5 pm. I also mentioned to him that I did not have a business phone and will I be using my personal phone or a business phone.

He said for now to use my personal phone and to write my number down. Now the trainer and another employee were there and asked for my number and gave me there just in case I needed to call or have any questions and after that we all went home. So I came in the next day expecting that everything will run smoothly. Now the Supervisor gave me my route papers and the keys to the truck that I was going to be driving. At this time there were other employees that were about to leave and go get their trucks ready and they were located down the street in a yard.

When I finally got to the truck that I was going to drive, I got in and the truck would not start. So I tried calling the other employees who gave me their phone number and they did not answer at all. Now the employees who were in the yard getting their trucks ready did not know anything about that truck not starting. So once they were done doing their pre-trip check. I rode back to the office to find out why the truck was not starting. So another employee stated that you have to turn the switch on the passenger side which was not explained or shown to me and he drove right back down to the yard. When the employee showed me where the switch was he flipped it and I thought it was on the inside of the truck but it was on the outside. So the employee was leaving and said that when I get down there to stop by so that they can adjust my brakes. When I finally got in the truck and was able to start it I tried releasing the emergency brake and the truck would not move, I tried working the controls and they did not work, I pressed my foot on the brake and it went all the way to the floor. Then as I was looking around the truck was so dirty on the inside and looked as if it was from the junkyard or Sanford and son show. It was so messy and had a whole bunch of trash with loose bolts and tools.

The truck had to have been at least 30 years old. So I decided to turn off the truck and walk back down to the office. As I was walking I already knew that I was going to leave and this was my last day. I was so frustrated and my day was starting late. Plus, I was also not going to ruin the plans my wife had planned for us and take a chance of getting stranded or the truck breaking down with no one to help me, especially when I tried calling the other employees and they did not answer the phone. When I got to the office I went to place the keys back where they set all of them. As I started to leave the Supervisor came out and I told him that the brakes, controls and truck were not working. He asked for the keys. I told him that I put them back and as he started to walk back there I got into my vehicle and left and headed home. I got home and my wife was shocked that I was home early. So I explained to her what happened and how my day had started. Then as I got settled in 30 min later Bill had been calling and wanted to know what was going on and to give him a call. He left a message and after that I decided to text him instead of talking on the phone.

I texted this message, "Hello Bill I got your message and I feel that this is not going to be for me at this time. It started off not going so well with the truck not working and doing things differently. I want to say thank you for your kindness. Have a good day."

He replied in bold letters yelling, "I DON'T KNOW THAT IT MATTERS TO YOU BUT THE AIR TANKS HAD NOT BEEN CLOSED. AND THE BATTERY DISCONNECT HAD NOT BEEN TURNED ON."

I replied, "Yea I wish somebody would have told me that when I asked for help. But nobody did not mention that and also it got frustrating going back and forth and getting the day started. When the vehicle was started I could not also release the brake to start driving and nothing inside was not working in the truck."

He replied, "Why don't you come over and we can talk about it."

At this point I did not respond anymore and knew that it was time to move on. So I decided to go on indeed and apply for some other jobs. And when I applied I got a response the same day and a recruiter called me and asked me some questions and then after the call said that she would forward my information to the hiring manager to set up an interview. I will say that God is good because I did this all in stepping out in faith. And the word says in (Deuteronomy 31:8- The LORD himself goes before you and will be with you; he will never leave you nor forsake you. Do not be afraid; do not be discouraged.) Now my wife went to get her nails done for the evening when she came back they were really nice.

Later that evening we decided to get ready. I went into another room so that I could be surprised what she was going to wear. I got dressed and when she finished getting ready she looked so beautiful. We left and she surprised me and told me that we were going to eat at Shanahan's, now that was surprising! When we arrived and got seated the waitress was very polite. I ordered a filet mignon and a baked potato with a salad, my wife got the same thing and it was delicious. The only thing that we did not like was when our food was brought out by the chef. He had an attitude that he either didn't feel like working or serving us our food, but the rest of the evening was fantastic. After enjoying eating, there was another surprise on our date and we went to a nice 5-star hotel for the evening and then got up the next morning and went home. That same week I got on the ball and started applying for other jobs and not just waiting for that other job to contact me back.

Now during that week, I was also waiting for my check to come direct deposit on Friday. That morning when I got up it did not show any direct deposit and that the company that used to work for stopped the direct deposit. So I got dressed and drove up to the job and eventually had a conversation with Bill and let him know why I left and that I felt I was not safe driving that truck that was not working and did not start up. He made the excuse that I could have come to him and that we could have figured it out. I told him that by that time 2 hours had gone by and I was just frustrated and getting a late start and that at this point I realized that this was not going to be for me.

After that he offered to see if I would be interested in driving a frontline truck since right now the position for the other truck was not available. I told him probably not. He stated that what you're telling me is that you no longer want to work here. I said yes and that it was worth the effort. Then after we finished conversing. I asked for my check. He said that since he had not heard from me that it was mailed out on Thursday night.

Now when I got home 20 minutes later Bill called me and asked me still if I would be interested in going for a buddy ride next week to see how I would like driving that other truck. He said that I could think about it over the weekend and to let him know. I told him that I would think about it and we can go from there, but in my mind it was already made up that before next week I was still going to let him know that I was not interested. So next week has come by and I am patiently waiting. Monday morning came and I did not get my check. Then Bill called me and I did not answer the phone and he did not leave a message. So I went ahead and texted him and told him that, "I had some time to think about it over the weekend and have decided not to do that other job, but thank you for the opportunity to offer the other position."

After that he did not reply.

Now Tuesday morning I checked my email because I get notifications of what is going to be coming in the mail for that day. Nothing did not appear to have my check so I drove up to the office which is around the corner from the building that I worked at which is their corporate location. The company is not a huge company, they are a private company that only has like 30 people working for them. When I arrived, there were two ladies in the office and I introduced myself and let them know that I was there to see about my check. One of the ladies stated that the check went out Saturday evening and not Thursday. So I asked if it was UPS or regular mail. The receptionist stated that it was regular mail and that it comes from the Colorado location here. I told her thank you and that I would be waiting for it and left.

As I was leaving I received a call from one of the jobs that I applied for, while driving I pulled over and did a phone interview and set up an in person interview for Wednesday, but when the lady was trying to set up the interview she said that she was having some issues with putting my information in the system and that it was messing up and can she call me back in 10 min. I told her that would be fine. At first I was thinking that this was a scam, but it wasn't because I received a notification in a text from the company stating that they were going to contact me, so it really was legit. So 10 min went by and the recruiter called me back. There was another lady on the phone that I got introduced to and she explained who she was and that she was going to take the call from here and get me set up for my interview for Wednesday. From all the questions that I was being asked regarding my resume and work history, we actually were on the phone for about an hour. At the end of the call the recruiter stated that after the interview depending on if I get the job she will contact me regardless. The recruiter also stated that I would have to take a urine test and also a hair test and would that be a problem. I told her that I was bald and that the only hair that I have on my body is my beard and if that would be ok. The recruiter said that would be perfect and to make sure not to cut it off because they would need 1 inch of my hair. After that we finished up the call and no later than 2 min I received the information by email for the location of the interview.

The next morning it was Wednesday and I did not see any check in the mail from the notification. So I got up and got dressed to prepare for my interview, I did not have to be there until 10 am. So before that time, I ended up calling the other job about my check and that I still have not received it, Because I was thinking to myself that this is a small company and if the check is coming from Colorado and they sent it out on Saturday morning then it should only take a couple of days not a whole week. Now I ended up speaking with the receptionist and she said that the check was mailed out and that they do not have control over that, but they do go through a third party and did I need to speak with Bill. I told her that if she can speak to Bill and see if he can contact the third party and cut me a check so that I can come and pick up my check and have them cancel out the one that was mailed.

The receptionist said that she would let Bill know and I told her that I would give it one more day and call back and we can go from there. At this point time had passed and it was time to go to the interview. I am praying and asking God for favor and praying for traveling mercies and that these issues with my check will be resolved. Now I got to the location and it was not that far to drive. So I entered the building and was introduced to the hiring Manager. During the interview we had talked for about 50 minutes getting to know each other and him asking questions about my background and telling me about the company. When we finished conversing, the hiring Manager wanted to set up a second interview to speak with the Supervisor and to come in at 6:45 am to 7:00 am and to just dress casual like jeans and a collared shirt. I was so excited that I told him I would be there at 6:15 am.

Phase 8

The hiring Manager stated that would be too early and if you did that then the other employees would frown on that (but he mentioned that in a joking way). So after I left and started to drive on my way I was thinking to myself that the other company was playing games and not sending me my check and that Bill was being spiteful because I did not want to come back. But when I got home I was going to figure out a way to maybe contact the Colorado Labor board and file a wage dispute. So I looked up the information on the internet and found out that when a company does not pay an employee for their wages it's a violation.

In the meantime, I started to prepare documents because if I did not see that notification tomorrow morning I was going to start making calls and giving Bill a demand letter for payment. Now I did all that preparation and was ready for the next day just in case, because mind you I have bills to pay that are a little behind.

Thursday morning is here and there is still no notification that I can see the check being delivered. So now I am getting ready to leave my house a little early to use one of my credit cards to get some gas. I pulled up to the gas station and the card did not work and came back declined. I was like what? Then I checked my bank account and it was overdrawn due to an electronic bill that came through. I was like you have got to be kidding me. I had the funds in the account before the account was overdraft. So now I was unable to get some gas and had to go ahead and drive to the same place from yesterday for my second interview.

When I arrived, I met with two Supervisors and the hiring manager had sat in as well on this interview. Now after finishing with the second interview, I believed it went well and was told that either way I will hear something whether I get it or not. As I was leaving the hiring manager stated that if I don't get the job to try again and he also said to me that you know what's going to happen next, I said, "What?"

He said, "After you leave we are going to talk about you." (In a good way and we both started laughing).

Then next after I left the building, I got into my vehicle and waited there and made a call to the credit card company to find out why my card was not working. They told me that the reason it was not working is because I did not make a payment on the due date which was one day late, I was like WOW!! I did not know that a credit card company could decline a card for not making a payment for one day. I was like I have always been in good standing and never missed a payment. The representative stated that this was how their company does it. I told the representative thank you and the call ended. As I was driving away from the building I started to just drive straight home.

Now I arrive home and explain to my wife how the second interview went and about everything else, even regarding using the credit card. She also was like I never heard of a credit card company ever doing something with that type of situation either and it was good to know. So now I am praying to God trying to figure things out because it's like if it's not one thing it's another. My wife asked me if I regret not staying at that job or giving it a chance to see if the other situation would have worked. I told her no because even if I would have tried that other situation, I feel that I would have ended up leaving there anyway, because there were too many red flags, for starters my safety was not valued and the insurance was going to be too expensive. I told her that I am just going to put it in God's hands and keep praying, the word says in (Isaiah 40:31 But those who wait on the LORD Shall renew their strength; They shall mount up with wings like eagles. They shall run and not be weary. They shall walk and not faint). God is good, thank God it's Friday. So long and behold guess what? The notification came through and it showed the check in the mail.

So now I am rejoicing and celebrating God for his goodness and on top of that I get a call from the recruiter that they want to offer me the job and can I go do my drug test today. I was like yes I can. After that the recruiter explained that she will send me the address for the testing location and to continuously check my email because there are some modules, compliances that I have to make sure I finish before my start date. Now I get up to get dressed and check my email for the closest location for the urine and hair testing.

When I arrived at the testing site, I was waiting and when it was time for me to be seen the nurse had me hold a piece of folded print paper up to my beard so that she could cut it off. The nurse cut off a huge thick piece and folded it up in some foil, which I thought was very interesting. From all the years I have done testing this was my first hair removal testing for any company that I have ever worked for. So after I finished up from the test site, I drove straight home and checked the mail and there it was MY BELOVED CHECK!!!! WHOO HOO!!!Now I need to make a deposit so that I can get back on track and pay some bills.

Sunday was coming up and me and my wife were going to the Football game to see the Denver Broncos vs New York Jets. So Saturday we got up and wanted to take the drive to see if we were going to park a little far and then call a lift because parking was $150 dollars. When we drove down there we did not see where we could park that far. We just decided that we will just have to arrive early and see if we can get one of the parking lots for $50 dollars and went ahead and drove back home. Sunday is here and we are so excited for the game now. My wife wore her Broncos gear, but I did not wear my Pittsburgh Steelers gear. I always tell people that even though I am a Pittsburgh Steelers fan, I will still root for the Broncos because I have lived in Denver all my life. I enjoy the teams we have in Colorado. But I am definitely a Denver Nuggets fan for sure, I like the CU Buffs, I like the Colorado Rockies that's it and that's all.

Now we get up early and read our word and listen to some worship music and then get ready, but will do communion before we go to bed. We decided not to go to church because we wanted to get to the Empower Field early. When we arrived at the Empower Field early it was crowded and people were scrounging around trying to find a parking space. We did end up finding one, but it was not $50 dollars it was $80 dollars and the parking place that we went to saw a tow truck removing a vehicle from the lot. The parking lot attendant said that people were parking without paying and that is why cars are getting towed. I ended up being able to get a close parking space which the walk was not going to be that far. Excited for the game and we got parked and started walking up this ramp. It was not that far up. The seats we had were in a good location.

After we got settled in we wanted to get something to eat and come to find out, parking you had to use cash no credit card, the food concessions you could only use credit cards and no cash transactions. The water at the stadium was $7.85, we got one bottle to share. For one Hot dog was $7.50 each, we got two of them and said that we will get something on our way home. All the food concessions, depending on what you decide to get, were really expensive. Now we are at our seats. The game is starting and the Broncos always start off doing good but then their momentum seems to always slow down after about the 2nd and 3rd quarter. The game was fun and watching other people was fun, people were really getting upset when there were bad plays, but when it was good it was good. The score ended up being 31-21 with the Broncos losing and the Jets winning. The next game that we will attend will be the Denver Broncos vs Kansas City Chiefs.

Now the second week of October I have been receiving emails and calls from the company that is finishing up my background. Everything checked out ok except there were 2 jobs that they needed W2's for because the Human Resources was taking a long time to call back so they could verify past employment. My start date is supposed to start this upcoming Monday

October 16th. Also, this weekend I am taking my wife on a date to go see Dotsero. After that on Saturday, we got invited to go to a Sip N Paint that we will be attending. This is going to be a busy weekend and then we will attend church.

UPDATE: So the weekend was good and church was good and then Monday came and I received a call back from the company stating that my start date was going to be Tuesday October 17th. The next day I met with the Manager and we went over some safety and signed more papers. After that he introduced me to some more people that I did not get to meet last time, but had a quick meeting. After that I ended up riding with the supervisor to look at the work that I would be doing for installations. We ended up driving to Boulder Colorado and then back to Denver, and then Aurora. As we were driving I got to know him and he mentioned that he was a basketball coach and has a side job helping kids in High School to get to the next level for college and getting scholarship offers from scouts. I told him that was good. He stated that this was his passion because he played basketball and his son played as well.

We got back to the office and the Manager gave me some more training to do. I finished up for the day and he asked if I had any questions and if not then I could go ahead and leave and come back tomorrow at 7:00 am. The next day was here and I started work and this day was more of a relaxed day because the Manager and the Supervisor had meetings for half the day. Now when they got finished the Manager informed me that I had to take an Electronic Body Diagnostic to record any issues that would protect the company if I was to get into any type of accident to make sure that the injuries either had come from me or the accident. And if it comes from the accident they can compare from previous and see what injuries would need to be targeted for recovery. Now in my opinion It is just mainly to protect the company. I thought that this was something new that I have not experienced at any company that I have ever worked for in the field of transportation. So I took the test and asked my Manager if I could get a copy of the results, especially since it's information that is going to be kept with the company. He said that he will look into it and get back to me. After that it was time to go home for the rest of the day.

Phase 9

Now when I came to work the next day I was told that I would be riding with another driver to see what they do and how they work. Now the person I was riding with his name was Row. When we were leaving the warehouse I did not know that our drive to different locations was going to be long. With this drive I learned a lot about Row. He told me that he was with the company for 4 years and retired from the military. We ended up making deliveries and getting back real late. My day started at 6:00 am and did not end until 8:30 pm at night. The whole week seemed to be like that and I remember speaking with the Manager and was asked if I could work 10-14 hour days. Especially because this was the busiest season.

On Monday I received a text from the Manager telling me that my uniforms were in and that once training was over then I would be working by myself and with a helper. The day was good and I was learning a lot from the employee Row. Once work was finished and it was time to go home I arrived at the mailbox and received back 4 letters from the jobs that I was fired from. When I got home I opened them up and the first letter was from Human Resources saying that they had looked up my information to see who I was and that they apologize that things didn't work out for me at their company and good luck on my new endeavors in the future. The second letter was from the Director of

Human Resources saying that they hope that things are working out for me and appreciated my time I had worked for their company. The third letter I received was anonymous and was not so nice. They mentioned that they did not care about me getting fired and so what that this happened to me and to join the club of the other people who got fired and would do it again if they had the chance. The fourth letter was also anonymous and was not so nice. Someone had mentioned that it was best that I got fired at the time because they did not need that many people working for their company and it was for the company's best interest to let me go. During that week me and my wife went to the game to see the Denver Broncos vs the Kansas City Chiefs. We were trying to sell our tickets because we were thinking that we did not want to see the Broncos lose another game and also it was going to be cold. However, we were not able to get rid of the tickets and they were really close seats at the stadium.

The Broncos ended up winning the game for the first time since 2015 beating the Chiefs 24-9 and after that it was definitely worth going to the game. When we went to the game we planned to just catch a uber there and back home. Getting to the game was easy, but getting home was a terrible experience. We had to walk all around the whole stadium to get to the section where there was a ride share. It was crowded and cold, coming to the game it cost $43 dollars and getting home was $113 dollars. I told my wife never again will we do uber next time we will just drive and find parking. When we arrived home we both felt sick and took a Covid-19 test and it came back positive. So we ended up missing a week of work. I was so sick that I texted my manager in the middle of the night to let him know that I was not going to make it this week due to getting Covid from one of the drivers.

He texted me back saying to provide results and to get better quickly. I provided the results and during that week me and the wife took another Covid test and it came back negative, praise God he is the healer! We ended up going back to work that next Monday. When Monday arrived and I went to work I made sure to wear a mask continuously every day. The Supervisor approached me and said that he could tell that I was sick from Covid because I had lost 15 pounds in my face. He also stated that he thought I quit and was not coming back. I told him that it would take more than getting sick to quit a job. So I continued my training and was told that I would be riding with a guy named Mandy.

When I first met Mandy, he claimed that he was a Christian and that he had worked for the company and been here for 5 years and was from Columbia. When we were leaving after loading up the items that needed to be delivered we prayed before we left and the day started off real good. We were talking about the Lord and songs that we liked. I mentioned to him that I was an Ordained Minister and showed him my license. It seemed after that he wanted to have challenging conversations about scriptures. Mandy is only 35 years old and I had to tell him that it was not about me and him going against each other over the word and that our jobs as Christians is to share the gospel and try to reach people who do not know about Jesus. He was coming off being judgmental when I mentioned that I liked Gospel Rap. He mentioned that he used to be a rapper and was delivered from wearing earrings and rapping.

I told him that was good and that I have a great relationship with the Lord and that it was fine for me. Mandy stated that he does not watch tv and that he does not allow his children to play any toys like spiderman, batman or those marvel toys. I told him that I remember being 35 years old and when I was speaking to people about the Lord as well and that I am a little bit more knowledgeable and older. We had delivered to a customer's home and the guy was African American. He said to the customer that he did not know if this was true but when a man gets with a White woman and not a Black woman, it's because the Black woman always wants to fight.

I told him that I have not had that experience because my wife is an African American and we have been married for 31 years and it also depends on the woman, not because she has to be Black because any woman can be like that and wants to fight.

The customer said to me that it was good. At this particular time Mandy had said something that was inappropriate. So when we left I asked him if he heard of any Spanish or Latinas pulling knives out on people when they get mad. He said that he was not aware of that. Our next stop we had delivered to a female customer who kind of opened up about her ex-husband passing away and Mandy mentioned to her that she needed the Lord.

The customer stated that her family knows God and that she has an uncle that is an archbishop. Mandy acknowledged what the customer told him, but the customer seemed offended. The next day we went out again on delivery and before we were going to make our first stop I drove to a place called Pilot where all the truck drivers go to get filled up on gas and other things. Mandy said that he was going to pray, but I told him that I already prayed this morning and plus I noticed that when he prays, he does it in Spanish and since I do not know what he is saying, I did not participate and did my own praying. Mandy knows how to speak English.

When we got to our first stop and I was working, I noticed that he was trying to rush me and start saying that I needed to work faster. After we got to the truck I had to check him and told him that since I am new and when I get on my own I will get a rhythm that works best for me, and if he feels that I am going too slow then he can do the work for himself. Now I also mentioned to him that the Supervisor also told me the same thing about when I get on my own I would have to find my own pace. We also ended up making two stops that were not on our schedule that had taken a part of slowing us down but I believe he just wanted to deflect because it was getting late. So one stop was a place where his friend works and another stop was to get something to eat.

When I mentioned this to him he was getting offended and said that he did not want to talk anymore. I was like oh well that's your problem. Then later on during that day he decided to mention to me that the Manager decided to have me work by myself with a helper. I was like ok and then when we were on our way close to the last stop I said to him that since he has been here 5 years that it was really easy for him to be fast and he can get things done quickly. I asked him when he first started who was his trainer and did they still work here. He stated that he could not remember, but I think he was lying because he was not being a good trainer to me. The helper that was riding with us did not speak any English and they were talking through the whole ride in Spanish, but it did not bother me because I was able to tune them out and listen to my Bluetooth.

Now the next week I started on my own and noticed that every day I have been getting home late. The Supervisor said that once I start on my own I will definitely be slow at first but until I get a rhythm I will start picking up the pace. It is now close to thanksgiving and things are starting to look good at this job. The Manager told everybody that they needed to finish their training before the week or they will not be going out on delivery. I brought it to the Manager's attention that I finished my training and he literally approached me and gave me a hug and said thank you. The Manager that I work for gives great communication and even when I started provided me the tools for me to get my job done. I noticed that he does look out for his employees and always ask if there is anything that we need as employees. I feel that I have found my niche here and believe this is where I am going to stay. I also noticed that all the employees work well together. The manager that I now work for does believe in God and treats everybody fair.

After finishing my deliveries when it was time to go home. The Manager provided a thanksgiving gift basket for all the drivers. I thought that was very thoughtful. Another thing that I wanted to share is that when I started going out on my own I was provided a uniform, a business cell phone and my own assigned truck. The manager also texted me today and said that he has been seeing and hearing good things about me and that to keep up the good work. Now besides the guy named Mandy he finally came to his senses and started realizing that I was not going to be putting up with his mess. But other than that, I still feel positive about the Job.

Phase 10

Now another thing that I like about this job is my helper. My helper is from Columbia and has a baby there and from what information I did get. He stays with one of the other employees at the job and does not have any family here. We get along very well and work well as a team. Even though he speaks Spanish fluently and when we communicate I have to use my phone to translate what I am trying to say. When we go on deliveries he makes sure that the back of the truck is cleaned and the next stop is ready to go. And when we get a tip, he will say in English, "Thank you God."

Everybody who is a driver has a Spanish helper that speaks Spanish unless they are a driver that speaks both. The next day was a fantastic day when we went out for delivery. We drove to Estes Park and I ended up running into 5 deer that were crossing the street. One of the deer that was crossing in front of me was taking their time so when I blew my horn the deer looked at me and I started to drive off. Then the deer began to follow me as I was driving slowly. The deer sped up and when I floored the gas to go a little faster the deer was running after the truck for only a little bit then it turned off into someone's yard and jumped over a fence and fled off. I thought that was very interesting because this has never happened to me, but was a great experience.

When we got back safely from the deliveries I realized that things are really starting to get better. But I know that with any job that a person works there will always be challenges and things that you will or will not like about a company, but you have to make the best of it and also put God first in order to get through everyday life.

The year is almost over and I have finally bounced back from all the failures and struggles that I have endured throughout my career and jobs. But this journey is not the end, it is the beginning. I am turning over a new leaf and want my experiences to help other people who may have had similar situations on jobs and throughout their life. I hope that people will get something out of this book and take something from this. The Bible says in (Ephesians 6 11 - 18) Put on the whole armor of God, that you may be able to stand against the wiles of the devil. For we do not wrestle against flesh and blood, but against principalities, against powers, against rulers of the darkness of this age, against spiritual hosts of wickedness in the heavenly places. Therefore take up the whole armor of God, that you may be able to withstand in the evil day, and having done all, to stand. Stand therefore, having girded your waist with truth, having put on the breastplate of righteousness, having shod your feet with the preparation of the gospel of peace; above all, taking the shield of faith with which you will be able to quench all the fiery darts of the wicked one. And take the helmet of salvation, and the sword of the spirit, which is the word of God; Praying always with all prayer and supplication in the spirit, being watchful to this end with all perseverance and supplication for all the saints.

Today was a good day for deliveries. I had to end up taking a third helper with me because the load was a little too heavy. We started out good, but it was really cold outside. So I noticed that as the day was going on the helpers were playing on the heater, like when it got hot they would turn the air conditioner on and when they got cold they would turn it back to the heat. So I decided that since they are going to keep changing the temperature I will roll down my window when they turn on the air conditioner. When I did that one of the helper's was like it's cold. So I pointed to the air conditioner and the helper changed it back to the heat and left it alone and that worked. Now since working here I forgot to mention that there were people talking about some of the Spanish people who work there that fluently speak Spanish and have broken English and do not speak that well. I do not like when people talk about others or try to belittle them in any way. So what I did in order for me to communicate with them is I would translate my English to Spanish on my phone and then they would do the same by translating from Spanish to English with me. But when I did try to communicate to them in Spanish I would say, "Mi amigo" (My friend) and they liked when I would say that to them. One day I was getting off work and was driving home and my back tire was flat and I could not drive on the rim. So between ten to twenty minutes later a car pulled up beside me and the guy rolled down his window and said, "Mi amigo (My Friend) needs a ride."

I said, "Yes and could you por favor (Please) take me to the gas station to get some fix a flat."

He replied, "Si."

But I had to translate with my phone from English to Spanish. His name was Jose and he took me to the gas station and back to my car and waited for me to get going and when I was finished I thanked him and gave him a tip (money) for helping me. He did refuse to take the money but I insisted. As he was leaving he said gracias (Thank you) and see you tomorrow "Mi amigo" (My friend). Now with this story it pays off to treat people right. Had I been someone else or somebody that was one of the people who were making fun of him or people who speak Spanish this would have never happened. Plus, I also believe that God sent this person my way to help me. Now this next week was a little hectic. I had driven up to Aspen and got stuck with no chains. I ended up calling the Manager to get some assistance.

The Manager was very supportive and asked if me and my helper were alright. I told him yes and he then provided me with a number to call roadside and to send him pictures of where I was stuck. I told him that there was no damage to the truck and I just stopped and stayed parked. He thanked me for doing that and not trying to struggle getting out. I called roadside and they said the ETA was going to be 2 hrs. After we waited for the allotted time the Tow truck came and pulled us onto the road and we then got back on track and continued my route. I notified the Manager that I was back on the road. He replied, "Be careful and will see you tomorrow."

The next day when I came into work the Manager wanted me to come and see him in his office before I left. I was thinking oh boy, now what? Hopefully it was not something bad. So I went into his office and he stated that I was not in trouble or anything and that I have been doing a good job practicing safety since I have been there and to keep up the good work and be safe. The Manager wanted to make sure I also knew the smith system. The Smith 5 keys to success. 1) Aim high in steering. 2) Get the big picture. 3) Keep your eyes moving. 4) Leave yourself an out. 5) Make sure they see you. I told him that I do know this and that I always use this method every day that I am driving.

The Manager said that was good and he also wanted to bring something to my attention. The Manager said that we will be having a Supervisor's role that will be opening up in a couple of months and that him and some other people had sat and talked about it and my name came up and what did I think about that and if I see myself staying with the company because we need good people and leaders as yourself. I told him that I did appreciate that and I do see myself growing with the company and will give it some thought. The Manager explained what the position would be and what I would be responsible for. He also said that I did not have to make any decision right now but to think about it and we can have this conversation at a later time. After I left the office I made sure to get some chains before I left. Now I know some people will be reading this and wondering why a person would get fired from all these jobs that they have had. I often wondered the same thing. But I also know that there have been issues that I thought about and remembered some people who may have gotten fired because of clashing personalities, hygiene, not being a buddy and hanging out after work and going to get something to drink. Now I am not a judge for people who do what they do and have had these issues or run into these types of scenarios or know somebody that you know or seen with these situations. It's just that this was not mine. I hope that throughout this journey that I have reached people and given some wisdom, knowledge and understanding. I want to thank you for reading this journey even though it has not been easy, but I am making it work. At this time, it is too early to tell what the next phase will be when I decide to accept the position at the job that I am currently at which will be continued. Below I have provided some insight on the different types of situations that can or may have been done on jobs.

Human Resources

Human Resources is not your friend and they are not on your side. They are for the Supervisors, Management, and everybody above them in the company, but not for the lower leveled employees. They look for ways to get rid of people when someone comes to the office or -makes a complaint.

That's how they take advantage of firing people and getting the Supervisor to do their dirty work. They cannot be trusted. The only thing they are good for is answering questions that has to do with your paycheck, benefits, sexual harassment of the company. They can never be trusted so beware. If you have any issues for any other reasons that I mentioned you may have to go outside of the company and contact the EEOC if it is a very serious situation. They prey on people who have issues so that they can get rid of them and then hire other people to take their place. This is how they keep their jobs for security. Nobody ever wants to talk about it even though it is true and is considered to be a cover up.

They will play head games with the employees by mentioning that they have an open door policy and to come to them about anything. It is set as a trap to get you fired to save the company. Their job is to make the company look good and to wean out people who they consider trouble makers. The troublemaker defined by them is someone who does not agree with them and voices their opinion.

The Saboteurs

What is the definition of a Saboteur? Someone who commits sabotage or deliberately causes wrecks. A member of a clandestine subversive organization who tries to help a potential invader. From my experience there have been people who I thought were for me and were really against me and plotting to bring me down.

On the job the saboteur has been the type of person who is set to get to know you and collect information for the Manager or Supervisor and report your every move. They tend to do this so that they can build a case against you to get you fired. They first start out pretending that they don't like the Supervisor or have something against somebody you work with to hear what you have to say about the situation and to get your opinion about that topic. Then they also will play on your feelings and make it seem that they are on your side and you can talk to them about anything and offer to buy lunch or invite you to go to lunch.

Saboteurs are a kiss butt and their main goal is to make you look bad out of fear that you could have the potential to get ahead. A situation that I have encountered was when I was working in a job and doing what I got hired to do. People would be overly friendly and fake. Pretending that they liked me. Always coming to my desk asking if I had any questions and observing my work to see if I am doing the work right or having issues getting my work done. When I did good they would search for something and add that I needed to do my work a particular way that did not make sense. If I was struggling there would not be any help or assistance and would want to have one on ones to write me up for performance issues.

This is a tactic that started to damage my career. When this has happened, I have been talked about behind my back and left out of conversations and meetings while being provided the wrong times and locations. My advice is to be careful of the people you associate with. Not everybody is for you. Sometimes in these jobs it will be hard to tell who is true or not. There are people who will be jealous of you and are not wanting you to succeed. Try to keep things as business and mind your business. Keep your conversations short and to a minimum. I don't mean be quiet on the job. If someone asks you your name tell them and keep it pushing. But if you have never had any experiences of someone being a saboteur and trying to get you fired then that is good. You have met good people like yourself.

The Critics

What is a Critic? It is a person who provides harsh judgements and finds fault in people. A person who likes to criticize and put people down and not take accountability for when they do wrong. But they always seem to recognize other people's flaws. They are always negative and have this chip on their shoulder that they can never do no wrong and are perfect. When you confront or ask them about themselves and their issues. They will deny or avoid the questions or not give a straight or complete answer.

Critics get off on creating a negative vibe and like to take the focus off themselves and put the focus on people who make mistakes and do not do things right. These types of people feed off the weak which gives them strength to the hopeless. They also like to take advantage of people who are not that assertive and cannot not speak up for themselves. Critics like to make themselves look good and feel good. When they get an opportunity to attack they will go in for the kill. Not to literally kill, but to take down. They also like to express disapproval of one's faults, condemn, punish, denounce, decry. They like to speak badly of everyone and critique them. There is a saying that says, "You will never be criticized by someone who is doing more than you. You will always be criticized by someone doing less."

If you run into people who are like that, the best

thing to do is to turn the other cheek and walk away from people with a negative spirit who really like to put you down, belittle you, or try to make you feel small. Be glad that you are nothing like them and are a better person who does not have to stoop to their level and hurt other people. Remind and tell yourself that you are a better person by the grace of God and that if God is for you, who can be against you. Don't be that person, but surround yourself around positive people who like to be around you. If you know somebody that is like that and they see you as nothing then you need to be nothing to them and move on. Understand that when people criticize it does not make them smarter or better than anyone or you, it's because being critical of others is what they do not like about themselves. Know this you will get criticized if you are successful, if you fail, don't give up, get up, for just being yourself and not trying to be somebody else. So no matter what you do, whether good or bad people will always have something negative to say and you will be criticized. Now if they are people that you work with, be careful about association because they want to know every move that you make to try to find something to use against you.

The Fearful Ones

What are the fearful ones? They are the ones that want to speak up, but they are afraid when they see that you are being done wrong. They are the eyes and ears and will know what is going on with everybody. They sit back and watch, and observe all situations that are in their presents. They shake their heads as if it's a shame what people are going through and never say anything to defend but do not have the courage to speak up or report what they have seen.

It was always said that silence is betrayal. If you have ever heard of people who don't stand up for justice or for what is right is betrayal. These types of people do not want to get in the drama and find ways to not be in it or do anything to jeopardize their jobs. They will stand back and pretend not to be involved, but be involved in what is going on around them. They also tend to sometimes be selfish, sneaky and noisy which means that they are always in everybody's business. Now with this type of person I am speaking regarding the corporate or business world of working with someone like this, however some traits of this type of person can be acted upon in their personal life. Recognize this person and try to avoid them if possible.

The Supporter

What is the Supporter? A person who approves of and encourages someone or something. It's also a person who is actively interested in and wishes for success for others.

A Supervisor or Manager that also wants to see their employees become their best on a job. The one who wants to see and help you further your career. A person who has your best interest at heart and not trying to bring you down or try to find something to fire you for. A person that always checks on you and makes sure that you are ok and will ask you if you need anything that will make things better for you. A person who has nothing to gain or want anything from you, but to see you win. Someone who sees your potential and highly pushes you in the right direction. Someone that will guide you and provide you good advice. Someone who is straightforward and tells you the truth if you are right or wrong. The person who has integrity and respect for you and others. Someone who is an advocate and will speak up and stand for justice. The person that you would want to be around. The person who is an example and a leader. Someone who has a love for God and loves the Lord. A person who knows how to take charge and knows how to make right decisions. Someone who is not judgmental, but is thoughtful. A person who likes to see people smile, laugh and be happy.